Crabapples

Life in the Coral Reef

Bobbie Kalman & Niki Walker

Photographs by Tom Stack & Associates

🌸 Crabtree Publishing Company

Crabapples

created by Bobbie Kalman

**For my mom, Liz Walker,
with a whole lotta love**

Editor-in-Chief
Bobbie Kalman

Writing team
Bobbie Kalman
Niki Walker

Managing editor
Lynda Hale

Editors
Greg Nickles
Petrina Gentile

Computer design
Lynda Hale

Color separations and film
Dot 'n Line Image Inc.

Printer
Worzalla Publishing Company

Illustrations
Barbara Bedell

Photographs
All photographs by Tom Stack & Associates:
Mike Bacon: cover (inset), title page, pages 7 (bottom left),
  14 (bottom right), 18, 22, 26 (bottom right)
D. Holden Bailey: page 7 (top right)
David B. Fleetham: pages 4-5, 7 (bottom right), 8, 14 (bottom left),
  15 (bottom right), 17 (bottom), 20, 24
Jeff Foott: page 28
Manfred Gottschalk: page 10
Larry Lipsky: page 12 (top)
Randy Morse: pages 7 (background), 17 (top)
Brian Parker: pages 6 (top), 7 (top left), 15 (bottom left), 16, 26 (top)
Tammy Peluso: page 3
Ed Robinson: cover (background), pages 19, 26 (bottom left)
Mike Severns: pages 14 (top), 15 (top left), 21, 25
Tom Stack: page 30
Denise Tackett: page 7 (center)
Larry Tackett: pages 6 (bottom), 12 (bottom), 15 (top right)

Crabtree Publishing Company

350 Fifth Avenue
Suite 3308
New York
N.Y. 10118

360 York Road, RR 4,
Niagara-on-the-Lake,
Ontario, Canada
L0S 1J0

73 Lime Walk
Headington
Oxford OX3 7AD
United Kingdom

Cataloging in Publication Data
Kalman, Bobbie
  Life in the coral reef

(Crabapples)
Includes index.

ISBN 0-86505-629-3 (library bound)   ISBN 0-86505-729-X (pbk.)
This book looks at several aspects of coral reefs, including their
formation, types of reefs, the reef ecosystem, and threats to reefs.

1. Coral reef ecology - Juvenile literature. 2. Coral reefs and
islands - Juvenile literature. I. Walker, Niki, 1972- . II. Title.
III. Series: Kalman, Bobbie. Crabapples.

QH541.5.C7K34 1996   j574.5'26367   LC 96-36374
                                                        CIP

What is in this book?

Rainforests of the sea   5

What are corals?   6

How do corals grow?   8

Building a reef   10

The reef ecosystem   12

What is a food chain?   13

Coral reef life   14

Crowded reefs   16

Partnerships   18

Colors and patterns   20

Daytime on the reef   23

After dark   24

Reefs in danger   27

Save the reefs!   30

Words to know & Index   31

What is in the picture?   32

Rainforests of the sea

Coral reefs are the rainforests of the sea.
Like rainforests, coral reefs are colorful
places that are full of life. Rainforests
are home to more species of animals
than any other **habitats** in the world.
More types of undersea creatures live
in coral reefs than anywhere else
in the oceans.

So many creatures live in coral reefs that
scientists believe many have not yet been
discovered! Sea animals that live in other
parts of the ocean often visit reefs to
have babies and search for food.

Just as the rainforests play an important
role in keeping the planet healthy, so
do coral reefs. Both trees and reefs help
reduce global warming by taking carbon
dioxide out of the air. Unfortunately,
people are destroying rainforests and
reefs. These two important habitats
are in danger of disappearing.

tube coral polyp

a colony of hard coral polyps

What are corals?

A coral may look like a colorful plant, but it is actually a group, or **colony**, of tiny animals called **polyps**. Polyps are simple creatures. They do not have a brain or backbone, and they cannot move from place to place.

Polyps live close together. In some corals, the polyps are connected to one another. They can pass along food to each other and send warnings of danger throughout their colony.

There are more than 2,500 kinds of coral, but only 650 build reefs. These corals are called **hard** or **stony corals**. They may be shaped like fingers, brains, or antlers.

Corals that cannot build reefs are **soft corals**. Some have a branching shape and look like trees or bushes. Others resemble flowers, nets, or fans.

brain coral

yellow soft coral

leather coral

mushroom coral

fire coral

How do corals grow?

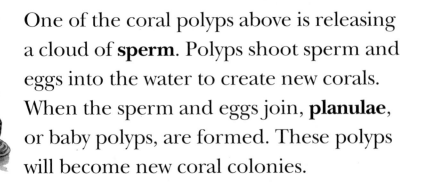

One of the coral polyps above is releasing a cloud of **sperm**. Polyps shoot sperm and eggs into the water to create new corals. When the sperm and eggs join, **planulae**, or baby polyps, are formed. These polyps will become new coral colonies.

A young polyp floats until it finds a hard surface, such as a rock, on which to attach itself. It then begins taking a substance called **calcium carbonate** from the water. The polyp turns this substance into limestone. It uses the limestone to form a protective cup around itself.

The polyp begins to grow. Soon it divides into a second polyp called a **daughter**. This division is called **budding**. The daughter grows and then splits into more daughters. In turn, they create even more daughters until there are hundreds of polyps living in the colony.

Cross-section of a hard coral polyp

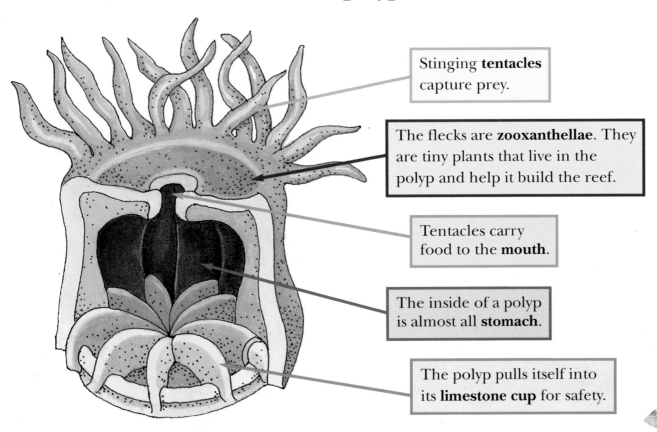

Stinging **tentacles** capture prey.

The flecks are **zooxanthellae**. They are tiny plants that live in the polyp and help it build the reef.

Tentacles carry food to the **mouth**.

The inside of a polyp is almost all **stomach**.

The polyp pulls itself into its **limestone cup** for safety.

Building a reef

The rocky parts of a coral reef are the skeletons of hard coral polyps. Living coral colonies grow on top of the dead ones. When they die, new corals build on their skeletons. Over time, the polyps leave layer after layer of skeleton, and the reef grows. Coral reefs grow slowly. It takes thousands—or even millions—of years for a reef to grow!

There are three basic types of reefs: **fringing reefs**, **barrier reefs**, and **atolls**. Fringing reefs form along shorelines. Barrier reefs are separated from the shore by a shallow body of water called a **lagoon**. An atoll is a ring of coral with a lagoon in the center. Atolls form away from land. Most atolls are found in the Pacific Ocean.

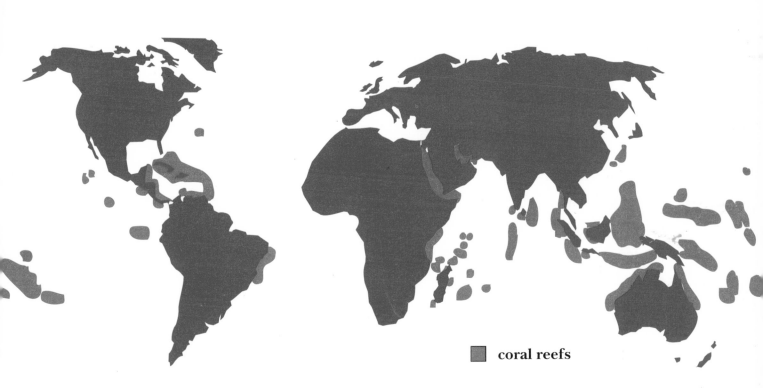

coral reefs

Coral reefs are found in the shallow parts of
warm oceans and seas. Hard corals cannot live
in fresh water. Reefs form only if:

the water temperature is between
73°F and 77°F (23°C and 25°C); corals live
in temperatures above or below these, but they
do not grow quickly enough to form a reef

there is enough sunlight for the
zooxanthellae to survive

the water carries enough food and
oxygen past the coral polyps

The reef ecosystem

Coral reefs are the oldest type of **ecosystem** in the world. An ecosystem is a community of plants and animals and the environment in which they live. The reef provides food and shelter for thousands of sea creatures that need one another to survive.

What is a food chain?

Plants get food energy from the sun. When an animal eats a plant, the energy is passed on to that animal. Another animal eats the first animal, and the energy is passed along a **food chain**. Tiny plants are the start of most reef food chains. They are eaten by very small animals, which are then eaten by larger ones. A food web is made up of many food chains.

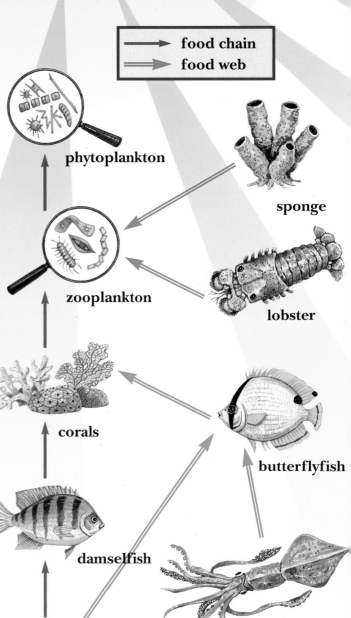

→	**food chain**
→	**food web**

phytoplankton

zooplankton

sponge

lobster

parrotfish

corals

butterflyfish

moray eel

pufferfish

damselfish

squid

barracuda

shark

13

Coral reef life

Triton's trumpet snail

Coral reefs are home to thousands of different creatures such as fish, sponges, worms, shells, sea anemones, sea stars, shrimps, lobsters, and crabs. Some predators, such as sharks and barracuda, hunt on the reef but sleep elsewhere.

bluecheek butterflyfish

whitetip reef shark

anemone

sea star

azure sponge

flatworm

Crowded reefs

Coral reefs are very crowded. In order to survive, each species has its own **niche** within the reef community. An animal's niche includes where it lives on the reef, what it eats, how it finds food, and how it defends itself against predators.

Some reef animals are covered with sharp spines that keep predators away. Others are flat or oddly shaped so they can slip into places where predators cannot follow.

Some animals live on the reef's surface, some hide in crevices, and others prefer to be on or near the ocean floor. Creatures that are active at different times often share a home. When one is out hunting, the other sleeps.

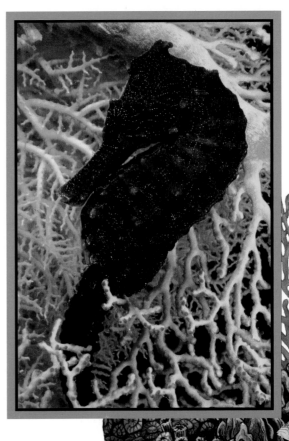

Partnerships

Some reef animals have partnerships called **symbiotic relationships**. Partners in a symbiotic relationship provide one another with food, shelter, or protection from enemies. Very often, one of the animals cannot live without the other.

The clownfish, shown left, always stays near an **anemone**. Anemones are animals with poisonous tentacles, which they use to capture prey. Unlike other fish, clownfish are not harmed by the stinging tentacles. They hide among them to avoid enemies. In turn, clownfish protect the anemone by fighting off fish that eat it.

Reefs often have several **cleaning stations**, such as the one shown below. At these stations, cleaner fish or shrimp eat small creatures that live on the scales of larger fish. Cleaners get a free meal and keep the skin and scales of other fish healthy.

Colors and patterns

A creature's colors and patterns may look beautiful, but they are also important to its survival. Some markings **camouflage** animals by helping them blend into the colorful reef. Several creatures, such as octopuses, can change their coloring to match different backgrounds.

Disruptive patterns, such as stripes, spots, and splotches, make it difficult for enemies to see the outline of an animal's body. **Eyespots** confuse an enemy by making the back end of a creature look like its front. Bright colors warn predators that certain prey taste bad or are poisonous. Predators know that creatures with red, black, or yellow markings, such as this nudibranch, can harm them.

disruptive patterns

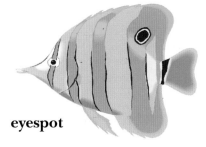

eyespot

Daytime on the reef

Daytime on the reef is busy and colorful. Thousands of fish hunt or graze on sea plants. Some escape from enemies, and others defend their area against intruders. Close to two-thirds of reef fish are **diurnal**, or active during the day. Turtles and snakes also visit the reef in the daytime.

Most diurnal creatures are brightly colored to blend in with the reds, yellows, greens, and purples of the well-lit reef. They have good eyesight, allowing them to spot predators or prey easily.

At the end of the day, the bright colors of most fish change to duller shades, which make the fish less noticeable to **crepuscular** hunters. Crepuscular predators are most active at dawn and dusk. They include sharks, barracuda, and groupers. As the tired daytime creatures try to get home, they make easy targets for the alert predators.

After dark

The reef looks very different at night! After the diurnal animals reach home, the reef appears bare and still. Other creatures soon emerge from hiding, however, and the reef is again full of life. **Nocturnal** creatures are active at night.

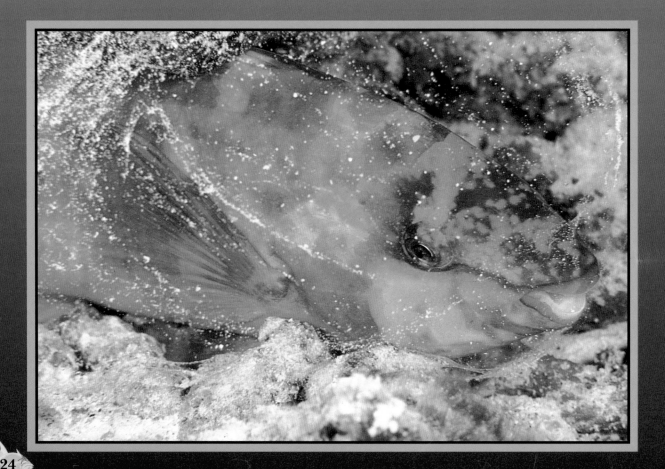

Coral polyps, worms, sea stars, eels, lobsters, and octopuses are nocturnal. Fish that eat these creatures also come out at night.

Some animals, such as the squid below, are **bioluminescent**. They create a glow inside their body. Scientists think that these creatures flash their light on and off to attract prey.

Reefs in danger

Even though reefs appear to be built of sturdy, solid rock, they are actually very fragile. Storms and coral predators damage reefs, but human carelessness may destroy them completely.

Storm damage

In minutes, a storm can wreck corals that have taken hundreds of years to grow. Crashing waves smash corals into bits, fling them onto the shore, or drag them into deeper waters where they cannot survive.

Too many predators

Predators of coral polyps, such as the crown-of-thorns starfish shown left, quickly devour large areas of coral reefs. They leave only the coral skeletons.

Recently, whole reefs have been wiped out because there are so many of these starfish. Some scientists think that the number of starfish has grown because people have taken away too many of their natural enemies.

Coral bleaching

Bleaching happens when polyps lose their zooxanthellae, the plants that live inside their body. The polyps turn white and can no longer build the reef. Storms and diseases cause some coral bleaching, but scientists think that the **greenhouse effect**, which has warmed the oceans, causes the most damage. Zooxanthellae cannot stay in a polyp's body when the water gets too warm.

Human carelessness

Humans have done a great deal of damage to coral reefs. Many divers touch, stand on, or kick living corals, causing the polyps to die. Boaters also kill polyps by dropping anchor on the coral.

Water pollution

Corals cannot survive in polluted waters. Sometimes boats leak oil or gas into the water. Cans, bags of garbage, plastic bottles, and fishing nets are often thrown overboard. Chemicals and sewage are also dumped into the water.

Taking too many fish

Over-fishing is a threat to the reef community. When people take too many of one kind of fish, they upset the balance of the reef ecosystem. Many of the fish are taken to be sold as pets.

Dynamite and poison

Some fish hunters dynamite the reef to stun fish and destroy their hiding places. Others shoot poison or bleach into crevices to drive out the fish. The poisons kill many fish instantly. Those that are captured for pet shops often die within weeks.

Catching many types of reef fish is against the law. The hunter on the left is taking protected fish to sell to pet shops. He wears a mask because he does not want to be recognized and arrested.

Save the reefs!

Healthy coral reefs are an important part of a healthy planet. Sea creatures need them to survive, but reefs are helpful to humans as well. The poisons of some reef plants and animals can be used to make medicines. Reefs also help slow global warming by taking carbon dioxide from the air.

Many countries have made their reefs **sanctuaries**. In a sanctuary, it is against the law to drop anchor, pollute the water, or hunt. You too can help save reefs by not buying shells, corals, or tropical saltwater fish. Even though it is illegal to take them from reefs, hunters still do so because people buy them. When people stop buying reef souvenirs, hunters will have no reason to gather them.

Words to know

budding The process by which a polyp divides into more polyps; this type of reproduction makes a coral grow larger

calcium carbonate A substance made of calcium, carbon, and oxygen

cleaning station A place where small fish or shrimp clean larger fish; large fish know where these stations are, and they line up to be cleaned

colony A group of animals or plants of the same species that live close together

crepuscular Describing an animal that is most active at dawn and dusk

diurnal Describing an animal that is most active during the day

ecosystem A community of plants and animals and its environment

greenhouse effect The name given to the rise in world temperatures, which scientists believe is caused by air pollution

habitat The place where a plant or animal lives

limestone A type of rock made mainly of calcium carbonate

nocturnal Describing an animal that is most active at night

phytoplankton Tiny, floating plants that can only be seen under a microscope

sperm Male reproductive cells; when joined with a female's egg, they create a new polyp that will form a new coral

zooplankton Tiny, floating animals that can only be seen under a microscope

zooxanthellae Tiny plants that live in hard coral polyps and help them build reefs

Index

animals 5, 6, 12, 13, 14-15, 16, 17, 18, 19, 20, 21, 23, 24, 25, 30
atolls 10
barrier reefs 10
camouflage 20-21
cleaning stations 19
coral 5, 6-7, 8-9, 10, 11, 13, 25, 27, 29, 30

ecosystem 12-13, 29
fish 14, 19, 23, 25, 29, 30
fringing reefs 10
food chain 13
food web 13
global warming 5, 30
location of reefs 11
people 5, 27, 29, 30
pollution 29

polyp 6, 8, 9, 10, 11, 25, 27, 29
reef threats 5, 27-29
zooxanthellae 9, 11, 27

What is in the picture?

Here is more information about the photographs in this book.

page:		page:	
front cover	The fish shown is a parrotfish.	15 (top right)	If it loses an arm, a sea star can grow a new one!
title page	This reef is in the Red Sea.	15 (bot. left)	Sponges are simple animals.
4-5	Reef diving is a popular sport.	15 (bot. right)	Flatworms spend most of their time in dark places.
6 (top)	Polyps may be as tiny as a pinhead or as big as a basketball.	16	This lobster lives in a reef near Hawaii.
6 (bottom)	These polyps have their tentacles out to catch food.	17 (top)	This fish is not hurt by an anemone's stinging tentacles.
7 (top left)	Brain corals grow only 2.5 cm (1 inch) each year.	17 (bottom)	Sea horses are fish.
7 (top right)	Soft corals do not make limestone cups.	18	This clownfish lives in the Red Sea.
7 (center)	This coral is near the Maldive Islands in the Indian Ocean.	19	Cleaner fish have black or bright blue stripes down their side.
7 (bot. left)	If touched, fire coral causes the skin to burn and itch.	20	This fish is well camouflaged.
7 (bot. right)	This is a type of hard coral.	21	Nudibranchs are snails without shells.
8	Polyps release sperm and eggs at night.	22	This reef is in the Red Sea.
10	The Great Barrier reef, of which this reef is a part, is so large that it can be seen from the moon! It is near Australia.	24	Parrotfish sleep in a cocoon so enemies can't smell them.
		25	Squids mainly eat fish.
12 (top)	This fish is a wrasse blenny.	26 (top)	This crown-of-thorns starfish is eating a coral colony.
12 (bottom)	This lizardfish is eating a smaller fish.	26 (bot. left)	Crown-of-thorns starfish only eat coral polyps.
14 (top)	This snail eats crown-of-thorns starfish. People have taken too many of them for their shells.	26 (bot. right)	Half of this coral is dead. The white part is skeleton.
14 (bot. left)	Reef sharks are great hunters.	28	This hunter is catching fish at a reef in the Philippines.
14 (bot. right)	These fish live in the Red Sea.	30	Buying souvenirs such as these coral skeletons threatens the survival of reefs.
15 (top left)	Anemones are related to coral polyps.		

1 2 3 4 5 6 7 8 9 0 Printed in USA 6 5 4 3 2 1 0 9 8 7